The Gruesome Truth About

The Aztecs

Written by

Jillian Powell

Illustrated by

Matt Buckingham

WAYLAND

First published in 2008 by Wayland

Text copyright © Wayland 2008
Illustration copyright © Matt Buckingham 2008

Wayland
338 Euston Road
London NW1 3BH

Wayland
Level 17/207 Kent Street
Sydney NSW 2000

Senior Editor: Claire Shanahan
Design Manager: Paul Cherrill
Designers: Fiona Grant, Jason Billin
Consultant: Anne Millard
Indexer: Cath Senker

British Library Cataloguing in Publication Data
Powell, Jillian
The gruesome truth about the Aztecs
1. Aztecs - Juvenile literature
I. Title II. The Aztecs
972'.018

ISBN 978 0 7502 5339 0

Printed in China

Wayland is a division of Hachette Children's Books,
an Hachette Livre UK company.
www.hachettelivre.co.uk

Contents

The Amazing Aztecs

The Aztecs were a rich and powerful people from the Valley of Mexico. They ruled over a great empire in Central America from around 1200 to 1520 CE. At its height in 1519, the Aztec empire contained over 200,000 square kilometres of land and 3 million people.

The Aztecs were farmers, warriors, traders, **engineers**, artists and sculptors.

▼ Aztec warriors fought with spears and shields.

▲ The Aztecs used dug-out canoes for fishing and transport.

Master builders

They built magnificent cities, palaces and temples made from huge blocks of stone.

Tenochtitlan, their capital city, was one of the largest and most beautiful cities in the world.

▶ The temple at Tenochtitlan was 60 metres high.

God of chocolate

The Aztecs worshipped many gods in their temples. They even had a god of chocolate! They used cocoa beans to make a rich chocolate drink.

Gruesome truth

Those are some things that you probably already know about the Aztecs, but in this book you'll find out the gory and grisly bits that no one ever tells you! Each double page will begin with a well-known FACT, before going on to tell you the gruesome truth about the Aztecs. Look out for these features throughout the book – the answers are on page 32.

▲ The Aztecs mixed chocolate with spices and even chilli peppers.

WHAT IS IT?
? Guess the mystery object.

TRUE OR FALSE?
Decide if the statement is fact or fiction.

Dressed to kill

The Aztecs made beautiful masks and jewellery from gold and precious stones like turquoise. But they sometimes used them to dress up prisoners who were killed as a **sacrifice** for the gods. The Aztecs believed the world would end unless they kept their gods happy – by feeding them with human hearts, blood and tears!

▼ Decorated knives were used for human sacrifice.

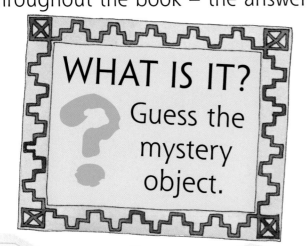

Spooks and Superstitions

FACT The Aztecs believed that every 52 years, the world might come to an end. They held festivals to try to stop this happening.

Gruesome truth

At the New Fire Festival, the Aztecs put out all the fires across the empire. Priests climbed to the top of a hill at sunset. When the planet Venus appeared in the night sky, they sacrificed a captive and cut out his heart. Then they lit a fire in his chest and new fires all over the empire again to keep the world alive.

▼ Fires were lit on the twelfth day of the New Fire Festival.

Ghosts and monsters
The Aztecs were superstitious and believed in witches, **demons** and ghosts. They thought spooks appeared at night as skulls to haunt people.

▼ Skulls were symbols of fear to the Aztecs.

6

The monsters and bad spirits that the Aztecs believed in took many forms. People told tales about spooky dwarf women and creatures without heads or feet that rolled on the ground moaning. They also feared monsters who wore necklaces and headdresses made from human hands they had cut off!

Death and demons

The Aztecs believed that most people went to a gloomy place called Mictlan after they died. Only great warriors, women who died in childbirth or human sacrifices for the gods were lucky enough to join the sun god or were re-born.

According to the Aztecs, ordinary people who died would go on a long and miserable journey that lasted four years. Their skin would be cut from their bones by a wind of knives and they would be chased by demons until they reached Mictlan, where they would just disappear!

▲ People believed in flesh-eating monsters.

▼ Dead bodies were buried or cremated. The ashes from cremated bodies were stored in decorated pots.

7

Hearts and Skulls

FACT The Aztecs made gifts and sacrifices to the gods.

Gruesome truth

They sacrificed men, women, children and animals. Most victims were prisoners of war. They were often well fed and looked after before the ceremony. Then they were dressed in special clothes and masks.

Human sacrifices

The sacrifice took place at the top of the temple steps so everyone could see. Four priests held the victim down and another one cut out his heart. They used knives made from **flint** or **obsidian**. The heart was put in a special vessel and burned for the gods.

▲ Decorated masks covered the faces of human sacrifices.

WHAT IS IT?

► Priests cut hearts from victims while they were still alive.

The body was then thrown down the temple steps before being skinned. The next victims were sometimes coming up the temple steps as the body was being thrown down!

Skull racks

The head was cut off and stuck on a skull rack outside the temple. The arms and legs were cut off and eaten in stews. The rest of the body was fed to the animals in the royal zoo.

▲ Some racks contained up to 60,000 skulls.

Child sacrifices

Children and even babies were sacrificed during special ceremonies. Aztec farmers thought this would please the gods and keep their crops growing. If there was a **drought**, they drowned babies for the god of rain, Tlaloc. They thought the babies' tears would bring rain.

▲ Young girls who were as tall as the **maize** were beheaded to keep the maize crops growing.

◀ A statue of the rain god Tlaloc.

9

Ball sports and Bungee Jumps

FACT The Aztecs enjoyed games and sports after work and at festivals. Many games had a religious meaning, too.

Gruesome truth

Their favourite sports included a rough ball game that often ended in injuries or even death!

Winners and losers

This ball game was played by teams of players using a hard rubber ball on a stone court. Players scored points by knocking the ball through goal rings high up on the walls of the court. They were not allowed to kick or handle the ball. They had to use their elbows, hips or knees.

It was a fast and dangerous sport. Many got bruised and injured as they clashed with other players.

Winning wealth

The winners could claim clothes or jewellery worn by spectators as their prizes. The losing team was sometimes killed as a sacrifice to the gods!

WHAT IS IT?

TRUE OR FALSE?
Aztecs played ball games with human heads.

▲ Players wore leather pads to protect them.

11

Birdmen

The Holy Birdman game or 'Volador' was a bit like bungee jumping! It was part of a religious festival to celebrate the Aztec calendar. Young men had special training to take part.

They dressed up as birds and climbed a 70-metre-high post. One sat on a platform at the top playing a flute and drum. The others tied ropes around their bodies and jumped off the post one by one. They each swung round 13 times, getting upright just before they hit the ground!

Bets on a board game

The Aztecs also enjoyed board games and gambling. Patolli was a board game, a bit like backgammon. Players prayed to the god of gambling before they began.

Some people gambled away their belongings, such as clothes and houses, and even their children!

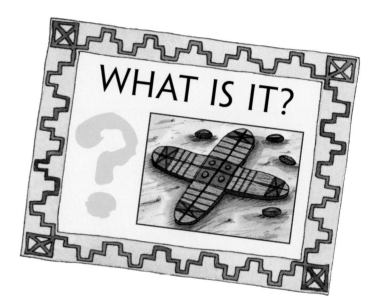

WHAT IS IT?

▼ They used cocoa beans with dots painted on them as dice.

▲ The birdmen 'flyers' wore costumes made from bird feathers.

13

Children and Chilli Peppers

FACT The Aztecs brought up their children with strict rules and punishments to make them good, obedient citizens.

Gruesome truth

If children were rude or naughty, they were sometimes tied up and left outside in the cold all night.

Births and burials

When a baby was born, the parents kept the birth cord.

But many children died as infants from diseases or accidents at home.

▲ A boy's birth cord was dried, then buried on a battlefield. A girl's was buried under the fireplace at home.

Child labour

Those who survived had to start working from the age of four. The girls learned to cook and clean, and the boys worked in the fields or hunted and fished with their fathers.

▼ Girls worked at home helping their mothers.

Childhood punishments

Sons of nobles went to school at the age of 15. If they didn't pay attention, the teacher punished them by pinching their arms or ears, or pricking them with cactus spines.

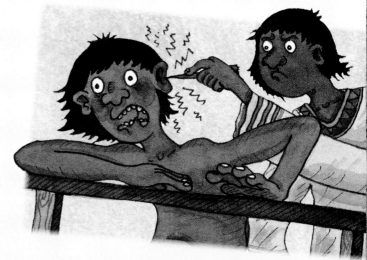

▶ Teachers also used cactus spines to keep pupils awake!

◀ If girls were naughty, they were given extra housework.

▶ The worst punishment for naughty children was being held over a fire of roasting chilli peppers, so the smoke stung their throats and eyes.

◀ If a family was very poor, children were sometimes sold to passing slave traders.

Royal Rulers

FACT Aztec emperors were kings, chief priests and heads of the army. They lived in grand palaces and ruled over the whole empire.

Gruesome truth

When nobles visited the emperor, they had to take off their fine clothes and put on cheap blankets so that they did not look as grand as he did! They had to enter barefoot, bow three times, and call him 'my great lord'.

Banquets and birds

The emperor's palace had rooms big enough to seat 3,000 guests for a banquet. It had its own library, zoo and **aviary** with ten rooms full of birds.

▲ The aviary and zoo at Tenochtitlan had nearly 300 keepers.

At each meal, the emperor was offered 100 dishes of food and entertained by clowns and jugglers. He ate behind a golden screen. Sometimes, the emperor was carried around in a chair with feathers to shade him from the sun.

◀ Wherever the emperor went, nobles swept the floor in front of him, and threw down cloth so his feet didn't have to touch the ground.

▲ No one was allowed to look at the emperor's face or turn their back on him. They had to leave the room walking backwards.

Maggots and Monkeys

FACT The Aztecs were skilled farmers, growing maize, beans, tomatoes, chilli peppers and other vegetables. Maize was made into cakes, pancakes and porridge and eaten with fruit and spices.

Gruesome truth

People also ate dogs, monkeys, frogs, tadpoles, lizards and insect grubs. Small, hairless dogs were bred for their meat and sold at the market. Ants, maggots, caterpillars and grubs were also considered delicacies.

TRUE OR FALSE?
The Aztecs used cocoa beans as money.

▼ Many kinds of animals and birds were sold live at Aztec markets.

18

Cakes and cactus tops

The Aztecs made special cakes from the green **algae** or scum they collected from the surface of lakes, which contained water-fly eggs.

At banquets, the rich sometimes gave their guests tobacco and drugs made from poisonous frog skins, cactus tops or 'magic' mushrooms that gave them **hallucinations**.

▼ Lake water sometimes contained chemicals from the whitewash used on houses, and gave people upset stomachs!

◀ The Aztecs used mind-altering drugs.

Drink and drunks

Alcohol was drunk at weddings and festivals. It was made from the **sap** of the **maguey cactus**, or from honey. But drunkenness was a serious crime. If anyone was caught drunk in public, they had their head shaved in front of a mocking crowd. If caught a second time, they were beaten to death! For nobles, the penalty was being strangled to death.

▼ To make alcohol from honey, girls swilled it round in their mouths and spat it out into bowls. The bacteria in their spit helped the honey **ferment**!

19

Feathers and Nose Plugs

FACT Aztec nobles wore rich costumes made from cotton, with fur and feather decorations, and jewellery such as earrings and nose plugs made from gold and precious jewels.

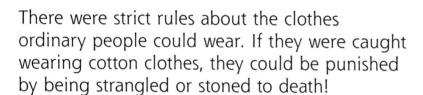

Gruesome truth

There were strict rules about the clothes ordinary people could wear. If they were caught wearing cotton clothes, they could be punished by being strangled or stoned to death!

Cactus and cotton

Ordinary people were not allowed to wear jewellery, and their clothes were made from cactus fibres rather than cotton, because raw cotton was so expensive to buy. They could also be killed if they wore long cloaks, unless they could show that they had battle scars on their legs.

WHAT IS IT?

◄ Only nobles were allowed to wear long cloaks.

Fashionable looks

Men and women painted their bodies. For women, the fashionable colour was yellow. They painted their faces with a yellow paste made from crushed insects. They dyed their hair black with mud or a deep blue colour with **indigo**.

▶ Women also filed their teeth to sharp points and painted them bright red.

◀ The Aztecs bound up their babies' heads so they grew into a flatter shape.

▶ Cross-eyes were thought to be attractive. Parents used string down the middle of the face to encourage them.

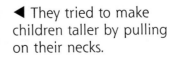

◀ They tried to make children taller by pulling on their necks.

Medicines and Mushrooms

FACT Aztec doctors used over 1,500 herbal remedies and knew how to stitch wounds and set broken bones.

Gruesome truth

They used a mix of herbs, magic and religion. They made powerful 'cures' from plants or mushrooms that sometimes sent their patients mad or even killed them.

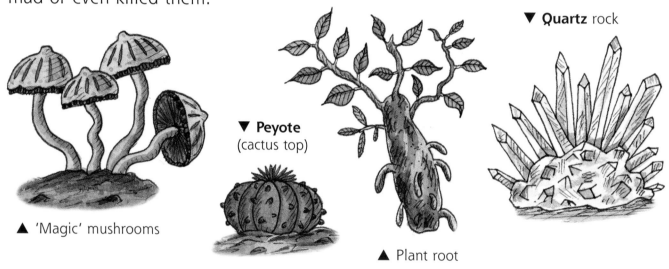

▼ **Quartz** rock

▼ **Peyote** (cactus top)

▲ 'Magic' mushrooms

▲ Plant root

Prayers and perspiration

Doctors sometimes gave patients drugs made from cactus buds that gave them hallucinations.

To mend a broken leg, they put on a paste of cactus root and lime and made a **splint**. To clean cuts and wounds, they used urine!

▼ They also mixed magical cures made from skunks' spray or quartz rock.

The Aztecs believed illnesses were caused by evil spirits, or were punishments from the gods. Doctors tried to drive out the spirits by making patients sweat in mud-brick steam baths, and by saying prayers and making offerings to the gods.

◀ If someone had a cold, they gave them a steam bath and dribbled dew from the fields into their nostrils.

▲ Herbs were used for healing steam baths.

▲ If someone had fleas, they painted on pine resin, then set fire to it!

▲ For earache, the Aztecs poured liquid rubber into the ear.

▶ If someone had taken anything poisonous, the doctor gave them a potion made from fried **chameleon** that made them sick at once!

23

Blood and Tears

FACT The Aztecs were a very religious people, worshipping their gods every day in their temples, and through ceremonies, work and play.

Gruesome truth

The Aztecs believed that the sun would die and the world would end if they did not feed the gods with human hearts, blood and tears.

▶ People began the day by pricking their ears with cactus spines and making an offering of two drops of blood for the gods.

▶ During ceremonies, priests pricked themselves with cactus spines to make their blood flow for the gods.

Aztec priests

Priests painted their bodies black and had red-rimmed eyes. They dressed in black, grew their nails long and did not wash or cut their hair. Often it was matted, smelly with blood and full of insects.

Festivals

Throughout the year, the Aztecs held festivals for the gods. At the spring festival, human sacrifices were shot with arrows and then skinned alive. To remind people of the new 'skin' the earth wears in springtime, the priests dressed in their skins. They taught that it was an honour to die as a sacrifice to the gods.

▲ Anyone who was sacrificed would live happily in the next life and might come back to earth as a hummingbird or a butterfly.

Fierce Fighters

FACT The Aztecs were a proud, warfaring people. They conquered enemy tribes to take land and **tributes** from them in goods and slaves.

Gruesome truth

The Aztecs attacked enemy towns and captured their people. Soldiers struck down enemies with fierce blows to their legs. They took their captives home and then killed them as sacrifices to the gods.

▲ Captives were fattened up as sacrifices to the gods.

War and weapons

The Aztecs fought in large armies of around 800 men. When armies met, they shouted out insults, then played **conch shell** trumpets and drums before the fighting started. They often began battle by hurling spears at the enemy using their long spear throwers.

Aztec warriors fought with knives, spears, arrows and deadly clubs made of stone with obsidian heads. These were sharp enough to chop off a horse's head with one blow. They carried shields covered in leather with feathers stuck on with bat-dung glue.

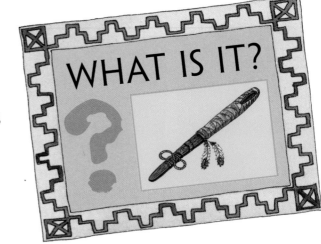

WHAT IS IT?

◀ Aztec warriors carried a range of weapons.

▼ Warriors who had taken
several captives won the right
to wear jaguar skins or eagle feathers.

Boy warriors

Aztecs saw war as a duty to the gods. When boys were 18, they took part in their first battle. Once they had captured their first prisoner, they became a warrior.

▲ New-born babies were given bows and arrows and children were brought up to fight.

▼ Boys had their long hair cut to show they had taken a captive in battle.

Costumes and captives

The more captives the warriors took, the grander their costumes became.

▼ To celebrate taking their first prisoner, young warriors had their faces smeared with blood from a human sacrifice.

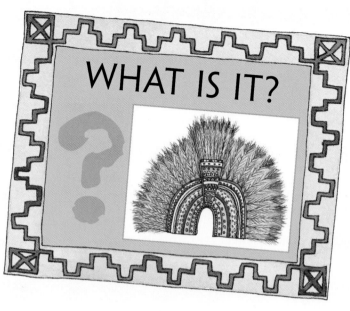

WHAT IS IT?

Even when the Aztecs had conquered neighbouring tribes, they wanted to fight them again so they could take more captives. They sent spies in to neighbouring villages who stirred up rebels to fight, but also found out their weak points so the Aztecs always won!

TRUE OR FALSE?

20,000 men were sacrificed by one Aztec emperor.

29

Glossary

algae	Tiny, weed-like living things that grow in water.
aviary	A cage or house for keeping birds in.
chameleon	A large lizard that can change the colour of its skin.
conch shell	A large, spiral-shaped shell that can be used like a trumpet.
demon	An evil spirit or devil.
drought	A long period without rain.
engineer	Someone who designs and builds the working parts of engines, machines or buildings.
ferment	To go through changes to make sugars turn into alcohol.
flint	A hard type of stone.
hallucination	A strange dream or picture in the mind.
indigo	A blue dye made from plants.
maguey cactus	A type of plant from Mexico.
maize	Corn, a cereal crop.
obsidian	A glassy type of rock made by volcanoes.
peyote	A dome-shaped cactus.
quartz	A hard, shiny material found in some rocks.
resin	Sticky stuff that trees produce.
sacrifice	Something given up as an offering to the gods.
sap	Juice from a plant.
splint	Something used to hold broken bones in place so that they can mend.
tribute	Something given as a payment or tax to the ruling power.

Further Information

Books

The Angry Aztecs (Horrible Histories),
by Terry Deary and Martin Brown,
Scholastic 1997

The Facts About the Aztecs,
by Jen Green, Wayland 2007

You Wouldn't Want to Be an Aztec Sacrifice,
by Fiona MacDonald, Franklin Watts 2001

Websites

http://library/thinkquest.org/27981/
www.mexicolore.co.uk
www.woodlands-junior,
kent.sch.uk/Homework/aztecs.html

Places to visit

The British Museum, London
Cadbury World, Bournville,
Birmingham

# Illustrator Note

The Aztecs were a great race that lived
a long time ago. They were skilled farmers,
warriors and builders who constructed
magnificent stone temples to worship
their gods. Looking at the buildings now,
it's easy to forget that they were once
covered in blood! Through illustrating
this book, I learned that life as an Aztec
was very tough indeed, but at least they
had chocolate!

Index

Answers

Page 8 What is it? A carved stone vessel used for storing the hearts of sacrifice victims.

Page 10 What is it? A stone ball marker. There were six of these 2-metre poles along the side of the court and they could be hit with the ball by players as another way to score points.

Page 11 True or false? False. Balls were made of solid rubber. But they were said to represent the heads of sacrifics victims!

Page 12 What is it? A board for playing Patolli.

Page 18 True or False? True. The Aztecs also paid for their goods with feathers and tools.

Page 20 What is it? An Aztec lip pendant.

Page 26 What is it? A spear thrower: a soldier held it through the loops so it extended the length of his throwing arm.

Page 29 What is it? The feather headdress of Moctezuma, the last Aztec Emperor. It was made with the feathers of over 250 birds!

Page 29 True or False? True. The Aztec Emperor Tizoc (1481–86 CE) had 20,000 men sacrificed when he defeated three tribes in battle. There were so many dead bodies they had to be thrown into the marshes.

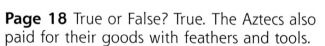

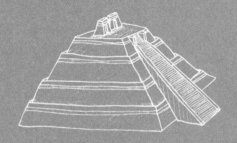